Fossil Fever

by Kathleen Weidner Zoehfeld
illustrated by Paulette Bogan

For Uncle Victor
K.W.Z.
For Vincent, Sonia, and Julie Song
P.B.

Special thanks to Paul Sereno,
Professor of Paleontology & Evolution,
the University of Chicago.

Library of Congress Cataloging-in-Publication Data
Zoehfeld, Kathleen Weidner.
Fossil fever / by Kathleen Weidner Zoehfeld ; illustrated by Paulette Bogan.
    p.   cm. — (Road to reading. Mile 4)
Summary: Jeff must learn patience when he accompanies his uncle
on an expedition to hunt for dinosaur fossils in the Sahara Desert.
ISBN 0-307-26400-9 (pbk.) — ISBN 0-307-46400-8 (GB)
[1. Paleontology Fiction. 2. Dinosaurs Fiction.] I. Bogan, Paulette, ill. II. Title.
III. Series.
PZ7.Z715Fo 2000
[Fic]—dc21   99-34417
                                                                        CIP

A GOLDEN BOOK • New York
Golden Books Publishing Company, Inc. New York, New York 10106

ISBN: 0-307-26400-9 (pbk)
ISBN: 0-307-46400-8 (GB)   R MM

Contents

1 / Convincing Uncle Roy

"New jeeps—check. Tools—check. Freeze-dried food—check."

Uncle Roy and I stood behind the Wye Museum of Natural History. Workers were loading supplies into two huge trucks. Uncle Roy watched, checking everything on his list.

"Medical kit—check."

"Gosh," I mumbled. "This checking stuff takes forever."

"Yes," agreed Uncle Roy. "But it has to be done. Once we're in the desert, our lives could depend on it!"

My Uncle Roy runs this museum. You'll never find him in his office, though. He's always zooming off to strange places in search of treasures. Next week he's leaving for a two-month trip to the Sahara Desert in northern Africa. He doesn't know it yet, but I'm going with him.

"Plaster—check. Lumber—check."

"Lumber?" I asked.

"To make crates for the fossils," he said.

"I love fossils," I hinted. "Especially *dinosaur* fossils!"

"That's what we're looking for," said Uncle Roy.

"I know," I said. "That's why I want to come with you."

Uncle Roy took his eyes off his clipboard for the first time. He looked me over. "You wouldn't have the patience for fossil hunting," he said. "You're too young."

I shrugged. "Gee, I guess I'll just have to sit around all summer."

"No way," said Uncle Roy. "While I'm gone, I want you to keep a journal of all the things you see. That's what scientists do."

"A journal?" I laughed. "I can see it now. Week One: Went to the park. Saw three squirrels. Week Two: Went to the beach. Found a clam…"

"Clams are amazing creatures," said Uncle Roy.

"Clams are clams," I said. "I want to see dinosaurs. I want to find the biggest dinosaur skeleton yet—a giant meat-eater, with teeth as long as carving knives and legs as tall as trees!"

"The biggest dinosaurs were
plant-eaters," said Uncle Roy. "The
long-necked Sauropods."

"See?" I said. "This trip would be
very educational for me." I knew that

would get to him. He wants everything I do to be educational.

"True," he said. "But we wouldn't have time to look after you, Jeff. And it would be hard work. Setting up camp, fixing meals, cleaning—not to mention searching the sand for fossils day after day and keeping a journal record of everything. We might not even find any fossils, you know."

"I'll find them!" I cried.

"And," he went on, "it's dangerous in the desert—snakes, scorpions, heat..."

"I'm brave!" I cried.

"You won't be able to take a bath or

wash your clothes for weeks," he tried.

"I was *born* for this!" I shouted.

"Okay, okay." He sighed.

I couldn't believe it! "Can I really come?" I asked.

"Well, I have to ask your parents, but maybe...*if* you promise to do your chores and stick close to the crew," he said.

"I promise!" I cried. "I promise."

Yes! I was really going to find a dinosaur!

2 / Off to the Sahara!

On Friday, Uncle Roy locked up the trucks. Their containers were being flown to Algeria where we'd meet them in a few days.

Monday morning, Uncle Roy and I and the nine people in our crew boarded *our* plane. We were on our way!

After we were in the air, I noticed
Uncle Roy was studying a map. "Is that
a map of where we're going?" I asked.

"Not really. It's called a geological
map," said Uncle Roy. "We know
dinosaurs lived between 228 and 65
million years ago. This map shows us

9

where to find rocks of the right age. No one knows exactly where to find dinosaurs, but maps like these help us make good guesses."

He pointed to a spot. "Right here," he said, "a scientist discovered the skull of the biggest meat-eating dinosaur that ever walked the earth."

"Bigger than *Tyrannosaurus*?" I asked.

"Yes," said Uncle Roy.

"Bigger than *Giganotosaurus*?" I asked.

"You do know your meat-eaters," said Uncle Roy. "Yes, even bigger than *Giganotosaurus*. It's called *Carcharodontosaurus*. That means 'shark-toothed lizard,' " he said, showing me a picture.

"Are we going to the spot where they found *Carch*-a-what-a-saurus?" I asked.

Uncle Roy drew an X on the map. "Here the rocks are from the same period as the rocks where *Carch* was found. That's where we're going."

"That's where I'll find my meat-eater!"

"Patience, Jeff. Once we land in Algeria, it'll take us about five days to get to In Gall," Uncle Roy said. In Gall is the little town where we planned to start our dinosaur hunt.

"Five days?" I cried. "This plane ride is long enough for me."

"Never mind," said Uncle Roy. "You'll be so busy keeping your field journal and doing chores, the time will fly."

<u>FIELD JOURNAL—DAY 1</u>

Drove all morning through fields and farms, then over the mountains and out into...SAND. I have never seen so much sand in all my short life.

At sunset we stopped. The wind started. It blew sand everywhere. Our tents flew. We had to chase them in one of the jeeps!

Scorpions must hate this wind, too—found one hiding in my sleeping bag! Yikes!

FIELD JOURNAL—DAY 2

Only—gasp—1,400 more miles to go. More road. More sand. Egads.

FIELD JOURNAL—DAY 3

Uncle Roy says I should write down everything I see. Sand. That's what I see. How long does it take to write that? Sand and more sand.

Did I give up clam watching for this?

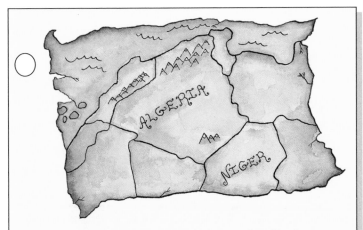

FIELD JOURNAL—DAY 4

We've finally crossed into Niger. Stopped at an oasis to gas up the jeeps and fill our water containers.

An oasis—that's what they call a town out here. I never thought I'd be so happy just to see some buildings and a few people!

Only one more day to drive!

FIELD JOURNAL—DAY 5

We're here! The tiny town of In Gall—a few low mud-brick houses, a dozen straggly trees, and a well with a trickle of water.

So, this is it. This is where I'm going to find the meat-eater that will make Carcharodontosaurus look small.

FIELD JOURNAL—DAY 6

All day we walked and looked. We looked at sand. We looked at rocks.

The hot rocks are wearing the

soles off my boots. The sand is making me itch. The water in my canteen is boiling hot.

I'd give <u>anything</u> for a cold soda!

FIELD JOURNAL—DAY 7, <u>8, 9, 10, 11, 12, 13...</u>

Must talk to Uncle Roy about this freeze-dried food—chili, chicken gumbo, seafood surprise. What's the surprise? It all tastes the same!

I'm going to keel over and die here. A million years from now,

scientists will discover <u>my</u> fossil
bones.

If the food doesn't kill me,
being bored will. All these days
and not a fossil in sight.

Nothing, nothing but sand.

There must be a better way to
find fossils!

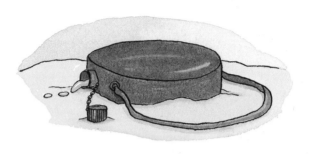

3 / Lost in the Desert

The next morning we were searching the same old hillside we'd looked at for days. I thought I'd do everyone a favor and scout out a rocky hill. I'd noticed it the day before.

The hill didn't look too far away. I filled my canteen and set out.

It was the biggest mistake of my life.

It took me three hours to get there!
Sometimes things in the desert look
closer than they are. I know that now.

By the time I reached the hill, my
canteen was empty. I was so tired, all I
wanted was a place to slump. But there
was no shade. It felt like the sun was
baking my brains.

I dragged myself up the hill and
looked around. I couldn't see our tents
or jeeps anywhere. I wasn't even sure
which direction I had come from. Lost!
I was lost in the Sahara Desert!

I hate to admit it, but I would have
started crying right then and there—if
I hadn't finally spotted my uncle. He

21

was way off in the distance, waving.

"Help!" I called, waving back.

He brought me a fresh canteen. "Don't wander off like that!" he cried.

"How could dinosaurs have *ever* lived here?" I shouted. "Nothing could live here! Especially not me!"

Why was I yelling at him when I was so glad to see him? I couldn't help it. Uncle Roy could tell I was getting a little worn down.

"I know this is hard," he said. "But try to be more patient. You can't just go wandering off. We all have to work together."

"But it's so boring," I whined. "I just thought if I tried out a different place…"

"Patience," said Uncle Roy. "You know what helps me? I try to imagine this place as it was 90 million years ago when *Carch* was alive—lush forests, broad rivers full of crocodiles, turtles, fish…"

"And clams?" I asked weakly.

"No clams," said Uncle Roy.

He helped me up, and we made our way back to camp.

4 / A Little Luck

The next day I tried to follow Uncle Roy's advice. I pretended I was walking under green trees along the banks of a cool river. I could see *Carch* on a hillside. He was stalking a herd of huge plant-eaters.... *Thump!*

I tripped over a rock and fell on my face.

The crew laughed. I couldn't blame
them. There's not much entertainment
in the desert.

I was sitting there rubbing my sore
foot when I realized the rock wasn't a
rock at all. It was a fossil bone. I asked
Uncle Roy to look at it.

"Good heavens!" he cried. "It's the

distal end of a femur!"

"The what of a what?" I asked.

"The upper part of a thigh bone," he said. "A *dinosaur* thigh bone. Excellent work, Jeff."

"Nah," I said. "I wasn't even paying attention. I was just lucky."

"Well, if some of your luck rubs off on us, maybe the hip bone will be nearby!" I'd never seen him so excited. He fell to his knees and brushed at the crumbly sand.

Then he shouted: "*Yes!* Looks like we've found your meat-eater, Jeff!"

"Why? How can you tell?" I asked.

He ran his fingers over the lumpy whitish thing he had just uncovered. "It's the hip," he said. "Nearly all meat-eaters have hips this shape."

Uncle Roy dusted his hands on his khakis and shook my hand.

"Let's excavate!" he cried.

That means we had to dig out the bones. We used some pretty amazing tools. There were little shovels that looked like toy shovels, little picks that looked like something my dentist might use, and little brushes the size of paintbrushes.

"Why all these tiny tools?" I asked. "Can't we hurry this up?"

Uncle Roy looked at me and raised his eyebrows.

"I know, I know," I said. "Patience, right?"

"Right," said Uncle Roy. "Fossil

bones can be delicate. We have to be gentle with them. As soon as we've uncovered a bone, we'll paint it with this glue. It will soak into the fossils and make them stronger."

"Whoa!" I cried. "Look at this!" I'd found a tooth nearly as big as my hand.

"Careful," said Uncle Roy. "After 130 million years, it's still sharp enough to cut you."

He brushed at the sand and rocks around the tooth and soon began to uncover a skull. "What a beauty!" he cried. "We might have a whole skeleton here!"

"How big do you think he was?" I asked. I lay down next to the dinosaur's thigh bone to measure it. It was longer than me!

"From snout to tail, I'd say about 30 feet," said Uncle Roy.

"Bigger than *Carcharodontosaurus?*" I asked. "It must be!"

"No. *Carch* was about 45 feet long and much stouter," Uncle Roy explained.

"Oh," I said, glumly.

"We don't always find what we're looking for," said my uncle. "But this is a great discovery! He looks like a cousin of the North American *Allosaurus*. No one guessed that this type of dinosaur lived in Africa, too!"

"Wow! Can we name him?" I asked.

"Sure," said Uncle Roy.

"How about—Sore-foot-a-saurus?" I asked. I was starting to feel pretty good about this.

"How about The African Hunter?" he suggested.

"Better," I said.

"*Afrovenator*," said Uncle Roy in Latin. "That makes it official."

FIELD JOURNAL—DAY 14, 15, 16, 17, 18, 19, 20...

The excavation has been slow. But since we started digging, I haven't felt itchy or miserable once. Uncle Roy says I have fossil fever.

I sketched this picture of Afrovenator after we had cleared

away his blanket of sand and rocks:

I like the way he's curled up, like he's been napping here for 130 million years.

Tomorrow we wake him!

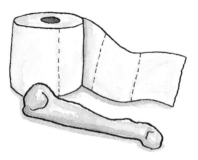

5 / Bringing Home the Bones

The best day of all finally arrived—the day we would lift *Afrovenator* up from his rocky bed and pack him into wooden crates for the long trip home.

The grown-ups lounged around, sipping their morning coffee. Meanwhile I admired my dinosaur.

"I'll start putting the bones away,"

I thought. I tried to pick one up.

"Wait!" sputtered Uncle Roy. "Stop!" He ran over to one of the jeeps and pulled four cases of toilet paper out of the back.

It was embarrassing.

"Uncle Roy," I whispered, "are you all right?"

"Perfectly," he said.

"Then, why...?"

"You'll see."

The crew all dived for the toilet paper. I just shook my head. They began wetting the paper and patting it around the bones.

Then Uncle Roy mixed up a batch of plaster. He showed me how to put casts around the bones, just like a doctor does when you break your arm.

I was a little nervous about it. But he let me wrap *Afrovenator's* skull, the most important bone of all!

"That's perfect," he said. "The paper

and plaster will keep the bones safe. As soon as the plaster dries, we can pack them in their crates. And tomorrow we'll head for home!"

FIELD JOURNAL—THE LAST DAY

The end of a hard day, and we're getting sand-blasted— AGAIN. I'm actually getting used to grit in my seafood surprise.

I can't believe I'm writing this, but I'll be sorry to leave this place. Who knows what other fossils are hidden in these rocks? Someday I'll come back here and find out.

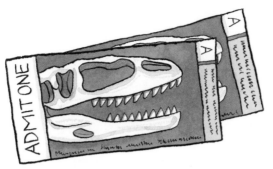

6 / The Giant's Skeleton Stands

Back at the museum, everyone treated us like heroes. Except maybe the preparators. Their work had just begun.

At their tables, they had all kinds of dentist's tools—picks, drills, you name it.

"Look at those tools!" I cried. "They are even smaller than the ones we were using in the desert."

"They have to remove every bit of sand and rock from the bones," said Uncle Roy. "Then they'll make fiberglass copies of the bones and put them together like a giant toy model."

"Must take patience," I said.

"Yeah, too much patience for me."

I stared at Uncle Roy. "But you're always telling me..."

He laughed. "They'll be working on those bones for a long time. I don't have *that* much patience!"

It took them a whole year, but the preparators finally finished the model.

It was worth waiting for. In fact, it was amazing! Crowds of people came to see it every day.

"What will happen to *Afrovenator*'s real bones?" I asked my uncle.

"Come on and I'll show you," he said.

Behind the museum, some large crates were being loaded onto a truck.

"We're sending him home," said Uncle Roy. "With a little luck, he'll soon be showing off for visitors at the museum in Niger."

I sighed as we watched the truck roll away. "I'll miss him."

"You know, Jeff," said Uncle Roy. "There's only one cure for fossil fever."

"What's that?" I asked.

He unfolded a new map and pointed to a spot marked with an X.

"Another trip," he said. "Want to come along?"

Author's Note

Although Jeff and Uncle Roy are fictional characters, their story is loosely based on the real discovery of *Afrovenator* (Af-ro-ven-AY-tor) in 1993 by Paul Sereno, Professor of Paleontology and Evolution at the University of Chicago, and his crew. *Afrovenator*'s model skeleton is on display in Niamey, the capital of Niger.